W9-BDO-210

# THE U.S. NAVY

In the early 1900s, sailors ate from tables suspended by ropes. When crew members were ready to sleep, the tables were removed and replaced with hammocks.

# THE U.S. NAVY

**Kathy Pelta**

 Lerner Publications Company ▪ Minneapolis

*To Edmond, once a Navy man himself!*

*For their help in providing information for this book, the author is grateful to Douglas Brookes, Curator, Treasure Island Navy Museum; Terry Cass, Nautilus Memorial Museum, Groton, Connecticut; Lt. Sophia Conerly, North Island Naval Air Station; Capt. Bill Hasler; AE2 J.J. Reyes, Navy Recruiting Station, Mountain View, California; Tom Teshara, Regional Director of the U.S. Naval Academy; Anna Urband and Ensign Lydia Zeller, Office of Naval Information, Washington, D.C.; and public affairs officers at Alameda Naval Air Station, Orlando Naval Station, Treasure Island Naval Station, and the USS* Lexington. *Special thanks go to JO2 Shawn Saucier and Lt. Cmdr. Doug Hocking of the USS* Carl Vinson.

Copyright © 1990 by Kathy Pelta

**Third printing 1992 includes updated information.**

All rights reserved. International copyright secured. No part of this book may be reproduced, stored in a retrieval system, or transmitted in any form or by any means, electronic, mechanical, photocopying, recording, or otherwise, without the prior written permission of Lerner Publications Company, except for the inclusion of brief quotations in an acknowledged review.

Library of Congress Cataloging-in-Publication Data

Pelta, Kathy.
   The U.S. Navy / Kathy Pelta.
     p.    cm.
   Summary: Presents a history of the United States Navy, describes how it is organized, and gives information on enlistment, benefits, officer training, Navy life, and the educational and career opportunities available to sailors.
   ISBN 0-8225-1435-4
   1. United States. Navy—Juvenile literature. [1. United States. Navy. ] I. Title.
VA50.P45  1990
359′.00973—dc20                         89-78209
                                       CIP
                                       AC

Manufactured in the United States of America

3  4  5  6  96  95  94  93

# CONTENTS

Shipyard workers load supplies onto a ship, using a motorized conveyor belt.

# Introduction

On a cold and drizzly September morning, a port in northern California buzzes with activity. A tender—a Navy repair ship—pulls away from a dock. It churns across the bay toward the open ocean.

In another part of the choppy bay, sailors in bright orange life jackets maneuver their small boat during oil spill practice. They stretch an oil containment boom—a string of buoys designed to keep an oil slick from spreading on the water. Fortunately, no oil has spilled. This is only a drill.

Overhead, a helicopter, or helo, roars past. It tows a minesweeper that skims the water like an empty dinghy. The bay is friendly territory. But the crew practices what it would do if the helo were flying over mine-filled waters. The minesweeper would help the crew detect explosives beneath the surface.

Still higher overhead, pilots from a nearby naval air station head out to sea for a day of practice exercises and submarine patrol. Land-based air traffic controllers monitor these flights.

On the deck of a carrier tied to the pier, sailors participate in a fire drill. It is essential that they be prepared for an actual emergency. As their leader explains: "On this ship we're one big fire department...if a fire gets out of hand, there's no place to run!"

On the other side of the pier, a carrier is getting ready to deploy, or cruise, for several months. Trucks rumble onto the dock with canned goods and frozen meat to stow, or load

**A Sea Dragon helicopter tows a minesweeping platform across the water to detect explosives that could be lurking beneath the water surface.**

onto the ship, for the voyage. Crew members, hurrying back from liberty, laugh and talk as they splash through puddles. A little water never stopped the Navy! Besides, where they are headed the weather might be even colder and wetter.

Every day, scenes such as these take place at Navy bases throughout the country and overseas. That is what the Navy is all about: ships and aircraft coming and going, well-trained men and women doing their jobs—on land, or at sea with the fleet. On the carrier preparing to depart, shellbacks, or veteran sailors, are not concerned as they settle in for the long deployment. They are used to it. Most sailors spend about half of their time at sea. But for the newcomers who have just come from boot camp, counselors will guide them and help them "learn the ropes." This term dates from a time when Navy vessels were sailing ships, on which sails were raised, lowered, and adjusted by ropes. In those days, a novice sailor literally had to learn the ropes.

# 1
# Our Navy's Beginnings

When the colonists began their fight for independence in the spring of 1775, they had no navy. So when England's warships blocked New York and Boston harbors to keep out trade ships with supplies for the colonies, the revolutionary troops could do nothing to break the blockade.

To get the muskets, gunpowder, and food his army needed, George Washington fitted guns onto the decks of colonial merchant vessels. He put soldiers aboard as crew and sent his makeshift navy out to capture English ships full of goods meant for the Redcoats. It seized over 50 ships, and was so successful that the Continental Congress voted to create a regular navy. Congress armed more trade vessels and ordered shipyards to build 13 fighting ships—three-masted, square-rigged frigates.

One of the first officers commissioned in the Continental Navy was John Paul Jones. At 30, despite a quick temper and a sharp tongue, Jones was a brilliant seaman. It was his idea to raid English trade vessels in the West Indies, in an effort to draw British warships away from the colonial coastline.

At the same time, Congress let owners of small, fast schooners and sloops become privateers. They had permission to seize English trade ships and keep the cargo as prize. The privateers did cut off supplies going to the enemy. But they also made it harder for the Continental Navy to recruit. Navy crew members were paid only $8 a month. Sailors

Captain John Paul Jones, who was born in Scotland, was a hero in the Continental Navy.

working for privateers earned twice that, plus a share in the take. They also had less chance of getting hurt, since privateers attacked only unarmed vessels.

As the war dragged on, Benjamin Franklin suggested the navy bring its fight to English waters. In 1778, John Paul Jones became a commander in "Franklin's Navy." During that year, he raided an English port, sank one trade vessel, seized two more, and captured a Royal Navy man-of-war. Officials fumed at "that pirate Jones." But because of his bravery and daring exploits, he was a hero to the ordinary folk of England. They wrote songs about him.

A year later, Jones took command of an old trade ship. It was not ideal, he admitted, but it was "the only ship for sale in France that will answer our purpose." He fitted it with guns and cannon and renamed it *Bonhomme Richard* in honor of *Poor Richard's Almanac*, Franklin's book that was all the rage in Paris. Then he sailed back to England.

Jones's clumsy craft met the English warship *Serapis* off England's coast on a September afternoon in 1779. *Serapis* was faster and had more and better guns. It hit *Richard* on the first volley, exploding two cannon and killing many gunners. Jones tried to board the English ship, but his boarding party was repulsed. *Serapis*'s big guns kept blazing. Its captain called out: Was the *Richard*'s captain ready to surrender?

John Paul Jones shouted an indignant reply: "I have not yet begun to fight."

The ships came so close together that ropes attached to a mast on *Richard* accidentally got tangled with *Serapis*'s bowsprit—the long pole extending out from the front. The vessels swung alongside each other, and Jones barked an order: Bring up the grappling hooks!

Held to the *Richard* by iron hooks, *Serapis* could not shake loose. With their guns muzzle to muzzle, the vessels traded broadside shots. When the sails of both ships caught fire, a truce was called to put out the flames. Then fighting resumed. The battle lasted into early evening. English farmers lined the shore to watch by moonlight.

Jones sent his Marine sharpshooters into the rigging to fire their muskets onto *Serapis*'s deck, and one Yankee sailor tossed a grenade into the ship's open hatch. The grenade ignited spare cartridges and set off a huge explosion. By now the decks of both vessels were gutted and burning. *Richard* started to sink. Still John Paul Jones would not give

Sailing aboard the *Bonhomme Richard*, right, John Paul Jones captured the British ship *Serapis* in a long, close-range battle.

The *Constitution*, center, was one of the first ships built for the United States Navy. After narrowly escaping capture early in the War of 1812, the *Constitution*'s crew won many battles, including this one, in which it captured two British ships.

in. It was the English captain who finally had to strike his colors, or take down his flag in surrender.

That 3½-hour battle helped to demoralize the English military. It also produced the United States's first naval hero. Naval historians have come to call John Paul Jones the "Father of the United States Navy."

After the Revolutionary War, Congress disbanded what remained of the Continental Navy. Founders of the new nation felt no need for a navy nor the cost of maintaining one.

A dozen years later, in 1794, members of Congress changed their minds. Pirates were preying upon trade vessels near North Africa's Barbary Coast. They demanded tribute money. When U.S. ships refused to pay, the pirates seized their crews and put them to hard labor. To fight back, Congress created a new navy, ordering six new warships and authorizing a force of 54 officers and 2,000 sailors to operate them. In 1797, the frigates *United States*, *Constellation*, and

*Constitution* were launched. Soon after, *Constitution* led a squadron to bombard the Barbary state of Tripoli and rescue U.S. sailors imprisoned by the pirates.

During the peaceful years that followed, Navy crews trained. They perfected their sailing skills. They practiced gunnery, tossing empty barrels into the sea for targets. When the nation again went to war against England in 1812, the Navy was ready.

Early in the war, *Constitution* was nearly captured. She was becalmed, or motionless, off the New Jersey coast, surrounded by five enemy frigates. Since there was no wind, her captain, Isaac Hull, had his crew tow her. The British did the same, using boats from all five of their frigates to tow their largest frigate, *Shannon*.

Then a breeze came up. Hull had his crew toss water on *Constitution*'s canvas sails. This made them less porous so they held the wind better. The U.S. ship surged ahead. After the wind died, Hull decided to kedge, or set an anchor to pull against. The crew spliced rope, tying pieces together to make a line one-half mile long. This rope was tied to an anchor, which the crew placed in a small boat. Crew members on the small boat rowed far ahead of the large ship to drop the anchor. Then all hands on deck reeled in the rope, pulling the ship to the anchor.

*Shannon* began to kedge, too, and was gaining. To escape, Hull played a trick on the British after rain began to fall. He hauled in his ship's sails. The British, fearing that a bad storm was due, did the same. But when rain hid *Constitution* from view, Hull put out the sails again and managed to get the lead he needed. After the mild storm moved on, *Constitution* was too far ahead to catch.

14

Good fortune and good seamanship made heroes of both the ship and her captain. In later fights, *Constitution*'s luck held. Because enemy shots seemed to barely damage the ship's outside planking, the crew nicknamed the vessel "Old Ironsides."

Other vessels of the salt water—seagoing—Navy were less fortunate. During one sea battle, James Lawrence was shot and his ship was destroyed. As crew members carried their dying captain to his cabin below, he begged them: "Don't give up the ship."

His plea inspired Oliver Hazard Perry, an officer of the U.S. freshwater Navy. When Perry met a British squadron at Lake Erie, he had Lawrence's last words sewn on his blue battle flag. After the British sank Perry's first brig, he had himself rowed to another, where he hoisted the flag and kept on fighting until the British surrendered. Then he sent a dispatch to U.S. forces on shore: "We have met the enemy and they are ours...."

**Rather than surrendering when his ship sank in a battle on Lake Erie, Oliver Perry went to another U.S. ship and kept fighting until his crews won the battle.**

**The Naval Observatory in Washington, D.C., tracks star movements and keeps precise time.**

Oliver Perry's victory on Lake Erie helped bring about peace in 1814. That same year, the Navy launched USS *Fulton*, its first steam-powered warship. By 1854, when Oliver's younger brother, Commodore Matthew Perry, crossed the Pacific to persuade Japan to open its ports to overseas trade, steamships were common.

During those 40 years, the Navy made other changes. It built an observatory in Washington, D.C., to track the sun, moon, planets, and stars. The Naval Observatory became the nation's timekeeper, and its master clock still keeps the official standard time. Navy scientists explored other parts of the world. They collected data and charted ocean tides, winds, and currents. During a five-year expedition, Lieutenant Charles Wilkes and fellow explorers mapped much of the Pacific and wrote 25 books on its people, plants, animals, and geology. They visited Antarctica and proved that it was, indeed, a continent.

A notable change in the 1800s was a stricter Navy dress code. Gone was the sailor's braided pigtail, kept stiff with grease or tar. New regulations required sailors to keep their hair neatly cut. But crews still wore the black neckerchief once used to keep grease off their collars. The Navy also continued to issue trousers with practical bell-bottoms—easier to roll above the knees when swabbing decks, and easier to yank off if a sailor slipped overboard. The short blue jackets they wore gave Navy enlistees a new nickname, "bluejackets." When the Navy turned to steam-powered ships, crew members no longer had to scramble up masts barefoot to rig the sails. Instead, they became coal passers, stoking the engine with fuel day and night. Now they wore shoes.

As the Navy replaced old sailing ships, it sold them for scrap lumber. This was to be *Constitution*'s fate until author Oliver Wendell Holmes wrote the poem "Old Ironsides" in 1830. It began: "Aye, tear her tattered ensign down." The words so roused people in the United States that they insisted their beloved Ironsides be spared. The ship was instead

When the Navy retired the USS *Constitution*, the ship was docked in Boston Harbor. The *Constitution* sails twice a year on "turnaround" cruises, during which it is turned around at its pier to keep waves and winds from warping its sides. Tours of the museum ship are given by sailors dressed in naval uniforms styled after those worn in the 1800s.

17

repaired and sent on a goodwill tour around the world. *Constitution* retained its Navy commission and became a museum ship in Boston Harbor.

Briefly, during the Civil War, there were two navies—Union and Confederate. Soon after the war began in 1861, David Farragut led a Union flotilla of gunboats up the Mississippi River through Confederate territory. Fired on from both shores, Farragut remained on deck. "Exposure," he said, "is one of the penalties of rank in the Navy." By then Farragut was more than 60 years old and had moved up through the ranks. He had served over 50 years in the Navy, having joined at age nine to become its youngest midshipman.

**Rear Admiral David Farragut stands at the helm (steering wheel) of the USS *Hartford* with Captain Percival Drayton in 1864, shortly after they captured Confederate forts near Mobile Bay during the Civil War.**

Neither the *Monitor*, left, nor the *Virginia* was heavily damaged in a three-hour, Civil War battle between two of the first ironclad vessels. From then on, new warships were built from iron.

Farragut's most quoted remark came when his squadron steamed into Alabama's Mobile Bay. The lead ship halted, even though it had a minesweeping device. The captain was worried about the mines—then called torpedoes—that floated in the bay. Farragut ordered his own sloop in the lead. "Damn the torpedoes!" he thundered. "Full speed ahead!"

In the Civil War, many Union ships were set afire when rammed by Confederate fireboats—rafts loaded with stacks of burning wood. After the Union frigate, *Merrimack*, burned to the water line, the Confederates turned it into an "ironclad." They covered the burned-out hulk with thick wood and metal bars and renamed it *Virginia*. As soon as northern spies learned what the South was doing, Union forces built an ironclad, too.

The Union's ironclad, *Monitor*, battled with *Virginia* the day after the Confederate ship rammed and sank two Union

19

ships off the Virginia coast. For three hours the ironclads clashed. The fight ended in a draw; neither could harm the other. But the Navy learned an important lesson. From then on, it built ships of iron, not wood. Iron gave more protection—and it didn't burn!

The Navy acquired its first overseas base in 1878 after Samoan chieftains granted the Navy the use of Pago Pago, a port in the South Pacific. Naval officers, among them Captain Alfred Mahan, pushed for more overseas bases. Said Mahan, a teacher at the Naval War College: "To be strong, a nation must control the sea."

**The Spanish-American War in 1898 began when a U.S. ship that was moored in the harbor at Havana suffered an unexplained explosion. Newspaper reports placed blame for the explosion on Spain.**

The Navy developed many more bases after a war with Spain at the end of the century. The war began soon after the Navy battleship *Maine* blew up in the harbor at Havana, Cuba, in February of 1898. No one knew who or what caused the explosion, but some newspapers accused Spain, which controlled Cuba at the time. Many people believed the newspapers' accusations. Chanting the slogan, "Remember the *Maine*," they demanded action. In April, Congress declared war. Four months later, the war was over. Naval squadrons destroyed the Spanish fleet in the Philippines and in Cuba. Spain gave up claim to Puerto Rico, Guam, and the Philippines and sold them to the United States for $20 million. The Navy established bases in these territories, in Cuba at Guantanamo Bay, and also in Hawaii, Wake, and American Samoa—Pacific islands that the United States annexed soon after.

## Theodore Roosevelt Modernizes the Navy

In 1901, Vice President Theodore Roosevelt became the nation's leader when President William McKinley was assassinated. Roosevelt loved the sea. He believed that his country should have a powerful navy to show a presence in the world.

"The American people must build and maintain an adequate navy," the new president said.

Orders went to shipyards for steel battleships, for sleek cruisers to be the "eyes of the fleet," and for coal haulers to supply the fuel. With more complicated ships, crews had more to learn. So the Navy set up a camp to teach recruits about steam engineering and the maintenance of electrical

Canvas leggings, called boots by people in the military, gave boot camp its name. Generally, the leggings are worn by new recruits and during special ceremonies.

equipment. Since recruits wore laced canvas leggings, called "boots," over their feet and ankles, the camp was known as boot camp. In 1902, the Navy began the practice, continued to this day, of giving to each recruit at boot camp a copy of *The Bluejackets' Manual.* This "bible" of useful facts covers everything from first aid and basic Navy customs to knot-tying techniques and abandon-ship drills.

To attract enlistees for Roosevelt's growing Navy, pay for sailors was raised. Meals were improved. Gone were the crackerlike biscuits called hardtack, the salted meat, and the daily ration of rum and water called grog. Now bluejackets aboard ship ate fresh meat, milk, eggs, fruit, and vegetables. The Navy began a recruiting campaign with posters that urged: "Join the Navy and See the World." Many people did! Even 14-year-olds could enlist—to play trumpet or drums aboard ship as "field musics" or "music boys."

In 1908, sailors did get to see the world. Roosevelt sent his Great White Fleet—16 battleships painted gleaming white—on a year-long global tour. The tour showed other nations that the United States had become a first-class sea power.

That same year, women became a part of the Navy when the Navy Nurse Corps began. Three years later, the Navy also had an official air arm. Early Navy pilots helped gunners improve their aim by spotting where shells fell during gunnery practice.

In 1914, Germany went to war with Great Britain and France. Although the United States remained neutral for a time, it sent Navy destroyers to escort British merchant ships. Nicknamed "tin cans," the destroyers protected the ships from German submarines while Navy planes and tethered balloons scouted for the subs from the air. (A German sub was called a U-boat, from *U-boot*, the German nickname for *unterseeboot*—or undersea boat.)

After the United States entered the war in 1917, troop transports and battleships steamed across the Atlantic to Europe. Back home, women took over many Navy jobs. To release enlisted men for active service at sea, the Navy signed on 1,275 women Yeomanettes to serve as office workers, recruiters, and fingerprint experts, or to do translating, drafting, and camouflage design. When the war was over the Navy disbanded the Yeomanettes.

With peacetime came other Navy firsts. In 1919, eight years before Charles Lindbergh's trans-Atlantic solo flight, a four-engine Navy "flying boat" became the first aircraft to fly across the Atlantic. The plane had a hull, shaped like a boat, for water landings. Also in 1919, electric potato peelers were added to ships' galleys to make preparing meals easier.

And that same year, Congress agreed to pay $25 million to convert the steamship *Jupiter* into an "aeroplane carrier."

*Jupiter* was originally built to haul coal. To turn it into the Navy's first flattop aircraft carrier, workers added a wooden flight deck that was the length of two football fields. Finished in 1922, the ship was renamed *Langley* in honor of aviation pioneer Samuel P. Langley. But to *Langley*'s crew, the new aircraft carrier was "Old Covered Wagon." Deck crews and Navy pilots used *Langley* to practice takeoffs and landings.

The Navy built two more carriers in 1927—*Lexington* and *Saratoga*. Named for Revolutionary War battles, these more modern carriers were nicknamed "Lady Lex" and "Sister Sara." In the 1930s, five more carriers were added to the Navy's expanding fleet.

Fortunately, all of the aircraft carriers were at sea on the morning of December 7, 1941, when Japanese aircraft attacked U.S. military bases in Hawaii's Pearl Harbor. But most of the battleships, destroyers, and cruisers of the Pacific Fleet were in the harbor. In less than two hours, 19 Navy vessels were sunk or damaged, 265 aircraft were destroyed, and 3,400 United States citizens—mostly sailors and Marines—were killed or wounded.

It was the Navy's worst defeat ever. President Franklin Roosevelt called December 7, 1941, "a day that will live in infamy." The country declared war on Japan the next day and on Germany and Italy, which were allied with Japan, three days later.

Admiral Ernest King, head of the Atlantic and Pacific Fleets, said, "The way to victory is long. The going will be hard." And the going was hard. Japanese forces swept across

Rescuers pull a sailor out of the water near the burning USS *West Virginia* shortly after the Japanese attack on Pearl Harbor. The attack on Hawaiian military bases is what led the United States into World War II, which had been fought in Europe for over two years by then.

the Pacific, capturing island after island. They seemed unstoppable. Although the Navy fought back, casualties were heavy. The Navy lost many ships, including *Langley*, which was hit by enemy bombers while ferrying fighter planes to Allied forces in the South Pacific.

Six months after the Pearl Harbor attack, Japanese and American planes clashed in the Battle of Coral Sea, near Australia. This was the first sea battle fought entirely with carrier-based aircraft. Surface vessels did not shoot at—or even see—one another. When a Navy pilot sank a Japanese carrier, his own carrier did not even know it until the pilot radioed back, "Scratch one flattop."

In June of 1942, naval intelligence decoded a secret message to learn of Japan's plan to attack Midway Island in the Pacific Ocean. Admiral Chester Nimitz called it "the biggest code-breaking operation of the war." Nimitz, head of the Pacific Fleet, made sure U.S. forces on the tiny island were ready when the enemy arrived. The carriers *Hornet, Enterprise,* and *Yorktown* steamed to the area. Their planes sank four Japanese carriers, a heavy cruiser, and many smaller ships. Japan lost 3,500 men—including 100 of its top pilots.

**Women entered the Navy as WAVES during World War II. After the war, women who wanted to join or WAVES who wanted to remain with the Navy were allowed to do so.**

The United States lost 307 men, the carrier *Yorktown*, and one destroyer.

The Battle of Midway was the turning point of the Pacific war. Japan lost its chance to finish the war quickly. The victory gave the U.S. Navy time to build more ships — especially carriers. Back home, shipyards turned out huge aircraft carriers. They converted cruisers, freighters, and tankers into small carriers by building flight decks on them.

Again, as in 1917, the Navy signed on women to free men for sea duty. Between 1942 and 1944, 11,000 women became "WAVES" (Women Accepted for Volunteer Emergency Service). They served in offices and communication centers. At air bases, WAVES used cockpit flight simulators to teach student pilots to fly.

As the months went by, American forces slowly won back Pacific islands that the Japanese had occupied. The invasions usually began when Navy frogmen — volunteer divers with UDT, the Underwater Demolition Team — swam underwater to plant explosives and look for traps. It was risky work. More than half of the UDT members were killed in action. Once the divers did their work, Navy ships bombarded the coast. Then amphibious (land and sea) craft — LSDs (Landing Ship, Dock), LSTs (Landing Ship, Tank), and LCIs (Landing Craft, Infantry) — put supplies, vehicles, and troops onto the beach.

Navy minesweepers and landing craft took part in the largest amphibious landing of the war on June 6, 1944 — D day — when the Allies invaded Normany, in German-occupied France.

By this time, several new devices made the Navy's job easier. Sonar (for *Sound-Navigation-Ranging*), allowed subs

**Military representatives of Japan boarded the USS *Missouri* in Tokyo Bay in September of 1945 to sign documents that made Japan's surrender official.**

to find enemy ships by the sound waves reflected back from them. Radar (for *Radio Detecting And Ranging*) sent out radio signals that were reflected back from objects far away, permitting Navy pilots and gunners to "see" in the dark or through fog and smoke, to locate enemy aircraft or ships. With radar, Navy destroyers could find the German U-boats that were menacing the North Atlantic. A third device that proved helpful was called "huffduff." It was an HF/DF high-frequency radio direction finder that let ships pick up radio messages and thus figure out a U-boat's location. Germany surrendered to the Allies on May 7, 1945. At Tokyo Bay four months later, a Japanese delegation came onto the deck of the battleship *Missouri* (the "Mighty Mo") to surrender.

With the end of the war, hundreds of Navy ships, including carriers and battleships, took part in a happier event—

"Operation Magic Carpet"—as they brought home millions of soldiers and sailors. This time, women didn't have to leave the Navy when the fighting was over. On June 12, 1948, President Harry Truman signed a law that allowed women to join the regular Navy.

Two years later, in 1950, the Navy transported troops across the Pacific when the United States joined other United Nations members in the defense of South Korea, which had been invaded by North Korea. Navy ships blockaded the Korean coastline to keep northern forces from getting supplies. Carrier-based jets attacked targets in the north. Navy and Marine helicopters hauled cargo and flew search and rescue missions. Although jet planes and helicopters were developed in World War II, they were not widely used until the Korean hostilities.

In 1965, Navy vessels again went into action, this time in Vietnam. Jets flew on bombing missions, using the carrier *Enterprise*—known as "The Big E"—as their offshore base.

Crews prepare to launch an A-4 Skyhawk attack aircraft from the carrier USS *Intrepid* off the Vietnamese coast in 1968.

**Technicians help astronaut Alan Shepard into his pressure suit during preparations for the nation's first manned space flight.**

During the eight-year conflict, Navy patrol vessels and mine-sweepers operated in Vietnamese waters, and the landing craft of what was called "America's brown water navy" patrolled the shallow Mekong Delta.

In 1990 Iraq invaded Kuwait on the Persian Gulf. Early in 1991, the United Nations voted to force Iraq to leave Kuwait. As part of this operation, the Navy helped the United States and its allies win a quick and decisive war against Iraq. It sent over 100 ships and 75,000 Navy men and women to the Middle East, the largest deployment of naval forces since the Second World War.

Navy vessels carried troops, ammunition, fuel, and other combat equipment to the Middle East. Ships and submarines launched missiles. Minesweepers cleared mines from shipping lanes. Navy pilots in A-6 Intruders and A-7 Corsairs flew attacks against Iraq from the carriers *John F. Kennedy* and *Saratoga.* The battleships *Missouri* and *Wisconsin* battered artillery units on shore with their 16-inch guns.

In relief operations after the war, heavy-duty Navy helicopters delivered medicine and food to thousands of war refugees fleeing the Iraqi army.

Navy personnel assigned to NASA (National Aeronautics and Space Administration) have played a part in exploring space since the 1960s. The nation's first space traveler was Navy Commander Alan B. Shepard, Jr., who shot 116.5 miles away from Earth in the space capsule *Freedom 7* in 1961. Ex-Navy pilot Neil Armstrong was with the spacecraft that landed on the moon for the historic moon walk in July 1969. Four months later, an all-Navy crew made a second lunar expedition. An all-Navy crew flew the first Skylab mission in May 1973. The astronauts lived and worked in the orbiting space station for four weeks before rocketing back to Earth.

That same year, 1973, female pilots graduated for the first time from the Navy's flight school. Three years later, women were allowed to attend the Naval Academy at Annapolis. By the 1980s, Navy women were regularly assigned to sea duty.

In December of 1988, Deborah S. Gernes became the first woman assigned command of a seagoing Navy vessel. Before Gernes completed the training that would allow her to fill her post as commander, however, Darlene Iskra assumed command of the salvage ship USS *Opportune.* The *Opportune's* skipper suddenly fell ill in December 1990. As second in command, Lieutenant Commander Iskra took over operation of the ship and became the first woman to actually command a U.S. Navy vessel.

Attack aircraft have become an important part of the Navy. Aircraft carriers serve as portable, seagoing landing fields for the fighter planes, jets, and helicopters that make up the Navy's air arm.

# 2
# Under the Water and in the Air

The first U.S. Navy vessels sailed on the surface of the water. By the start of the 20th century, the Navy had craft that could travel under the surface. Soon after, Navy planes provided ships with far-seeing "eyes" in the air.

## Submarines, the Navy's "Silent Service"

Very briefly during the Revolutionary War the Continental Navy had a tiny submarine called *American Turtle*. It looked like a big walnut shell. A person sat inside, cranking propellers to make the craft go up or straight ahead, and pushing foot pedals to go down. The Navy tried to use this craft to blow up an English ship, but the mission was unsuccessful. Soon after, the sub was destroyed.

In 1900, the Navy bought its first "modern" submarine—a cigar-shaped vessel that was 52 feet long. Soon other submarines were added to the fleet. All of them were powered by gasoline engines when they were on the surface, and by batteries when they were submerged. But the gasoline produced deadly fumes and frequently caused explosions. By 1905, duty in the Navy's submarine force was so hazardous that President Theodore Roosevelt ordered extra pay for the crews that served on these underwater vessels.

Through the years, submarine designs were improved.

Periscopes let submerged crews see ships on the surface. Gyrocompasses helped them navigate. Diesel engines replaced gasoline engines.

Even with the safer diesel fuel, submarine duty during World War II was rough. Water was in short supply. There was no storage space, and crews could distill, or purify, only small amounts of seawater at a time. Only cooks and bakers, because they handled food, were allowed to bathe regularly. Inside subs, the air was stuffy, and the space was so crowded that sailors slept next to torpedoes. Everything smelled of diesel, including the crew. The weather was unbearably hot for those serving in the South Pacific. For those serving in Alaska, the weather was miserably cold. Casualties among troops serving aboard submarines were heavy. Of the Navy's 288 subs in World War II, 52 were destroyed, and 3,505 crew members were killed.

A serious problem for U.S. submarines was that they had to stay above water when their engines were running. Diesel engines need air to function. German U-boats used snorkels to get air, so they could run their diesel engines while submerged and stay below the surface for a long time. The U.S. subs had to run on batteries when submerged. Every 48 hours, they had to come to the surface to run the engines and recharge the batteries.

After the war, Navy Captain Hyman Rickover began a campaign to run submarines with nuclear energy. Rickover, called the "Father of the Atomic Submarine," had studied nuclear physics. He knew that when atoms were split, they made tremendous heat. So why not let this heat convert water into steam? Besides running a sub's engine it would provide power for other purposes—air-conditioning, distilling

Hyman Rickover was instrumental in bringing nuclear power to the Navy. A captain while he was pushing for the Navy's first nuclear-powered submarine, Rickover was eventually promoted to admiral.

seawater to make fresh water, and separating oxygen from seawater to create fresh air. The small amount of uranium needed to split atoms took far less space than hundreds of thousands of gallons of diesel oil.

Many admirals did not agree that nuclear-powered submarines were the super weapons of the future. That did not deter Rickover. Over their objections and with the support of a couple of high-ranking government officials, he planned the first nuclear submarine. In 1954, USS *Nautilus* was launched. Right away, the submarine began to set records. It traveled 1,300 miles, while submerged, from Connecticut to Puerto Rico. Four years later, on August 3, 1958, *Nautilus* dived under the floating ice of the Arctic Circle to cross under the North Pole. For Commander William R. Anderson and his crew, there were special problems. Because they were under the ice, they could not use stars or the sun for navigation. Because they were so close to the magnetic pole, they found a compass to be useless. They had to rely on charts. But they made it! Afterward, New York City held a celebration and parade to welcome home the *Nautilus* crew.

Meanwhile, other nuclear subs began to set records. Also in 1958, *Seawolf* made a dive that lasted 60 days. In 1959,

**The submarine *Nautilus* gets a special welcome in New York Harbor as tugboats spray water in celebration. The *Nautilus* had just made the first voyage under the arctic ice.**

**The USS *Skate* was the first submarine to break through the ice at the North Pole. The expedition took place 50 years after Robert Peary's group was the first to reach the pole by dogsled.**

USS *Skate* not only went under the North Pole, it successfully broke through the ice according to plan! Its crew was lucky. The sub found a thin spot in ice that, in some places, was 25 feet thick. Even so, *Skate* surfaced slowly so ice would not damage its hull. In a light-hearted ceremony, crew members received special certificates for crossing the Arctic Circle and for going around the world (which they claimed to have done by circling the Pole from a mile away).

A year later, the nuclear-powered *Triton* became the first sub to circle the globe completely underwater, covering 36,000 miles in 84 days.

An Ohio-class submarine. The Navy orders several ships and submarines of the same design. The first of its particular design, *Ohio* became the largest submarine in the Navy. Other submarines of the same design are known as Ohio-class subs.

Submarines had always been fearsome in time of war. They hid deep in the water to sneak up on the enemy—unseen and unheard until their torpedoes struck their targets. Nuclear subs are more fearsome still, fast and quiet and with a thousand times the endurance of World War II submarines. And they are larger. *Ohio*, the Navy's longest sub when it was launched in 1982, measures 560 feet—almost the length of 13 railroad boxcars linked together! Modern subs do not need to come up for fresh air or water. They can stay down as long as their food holds out—and as long as the crew can stand it!

Modern Navy missile subs have two complete crews, each with a dozen officers and a hundred or so men. (Women are not assigned to submarine duty.) While the "blue" crew goes to sea, the "gold" crew has shore duty for three months—

A Navy captain, center, commands a submarine from the sail as it comes into port. The sail is the large, finlike structure that protrudes from the top of the submarine.

with time for "R and R." To most service men and women, that stands for "Rest and Recreation." To a submarine crew, it means "Rest and Retraining." Crews practice constantly, whether ashore or at sea. Crew members learn not only their own jobs, but a shipmate's, too. For example, the electrician's mate has to be able to fire a torpedo, and the torpedoman has to be able to change batteries! On a sub, crew members study the fathometer to see how deep they are. They check water temperature and the contour of the sea bottom. They monitor the nuclear reactors. During practice exercises, they fire missiles.

On a submarine, crew members have to assume the enemy is always lurking, always listening. During an actual "war warning" they must stay silent for days. They talk softly and wear soft-soled slippers to muffle the sound of footsteps. They are careful not to drop anything that could clank onto the deck to alert enemy ships, planes, or submarines to their location.

Modern submarines are more comfortable than earlier ones. Air conditioners filter the air and keep an even temperature. Bunks for the crews are arranged in tiers of three. Each bunk is screened off on three sides and has a reading light. In the skipper's stateroom, there is space for a folding bunk, a table with seats, a built-in desk, and an easy chair. Ships that deliver mail to submarines on patrol also bring supplies of fresh food. The submarine's eating area can be converted into a theater so crew members can watch movies or videos. Subs have libraries, game rooms, and even small gyms with equipment for exercise and in-place jogging. Sailors can run several miles a day, if they wish. With no shortage of water, after jogging they can enjoy a hot shower.

Eugene Ely takes off from the deck of the USS *Birmingham* in the first flight that used a ship as a runway.

## *The Navy's Air Arm*

Shortly before the Navy's air arm became official, in 1911, civilian pilot Eugene Ely made two historic flights using ships as runways. In New York in November 1910, he took off in his Curtiss biplane from the deck of the USS *Birmingham*. Two months later, in an even trickier experiment, Ely landed on a platform rigged on the deck of the battleship *Pennsylvania* in San Francisco Bay. A hook hung from his plane, ready to snag one of the 12 wires stretched across the landing platform. Ely swooped low. He missed the first 11 wires. But the hook caught on the 12th, and the plane jerked to a stop.

41

An S-3A Viking aircraft flies above its carrier, the USS *Dwight D. Eisenhower.* The Navy has come to rely on aircraft carriers and the aircraft that the carriers support.

Thirty years later, Navy carriers and aircraft became the backbone of the fleet. Following the attack on Pearl Harbor in 1941, carriers and carrier-based aircraft helped the United States win many World War II battles in the Pacific Ocean. As recently as 1990, the Navy's 15 aircraft carriers were still an essential part of its fighting force.

Although Congress has ruled that women may serve in combat squadrons (including carrier squadrons) only on a temporary basis, women pilots do ferry aircraft and deliver people and equipment to and from carriers. They may also serve full time on the carrier USS *Forrestal,* since it is used only for training and never sees combat.

Except on weekends, *Forrestal* sails in the Gulf of Mexico, steaming at 30 knots (30 nautical miles per hour, or 34½ land miles per hour) while student pilots practice takeoffs and landings. Ashore, these students have already done practice approaches onto a "flight deck" painted on the runway of an airfield. But touching down on a make-believe aircraft carrier deck is not the same as the real thing!

Even seasoned aviators find landing on a flattop to be a challenge. Night landings are harder yet. Pilots use a special landing mirror to get set for a perfect landing. They try to keep a spot of light, which they call the meatball, centered on the mirror. As the plane comes in low, a tailhook grabs the arresting wire. With a tooth-crunching jolt, the plane slows from 150 miles per hour to nothing in two seconds.

**Flight deck crew members prepare an F-14A Tomcat aircraft for takeoff. The different colored shirts worn by the crew members indicate the specific job each person has.**

Only a seat belt and shoulder harness keep the pilot from shooting through the windscreen.

In case anything goes wrong, crash emergency vehicles and firefighters are always standing by. Overhead, a helicopter hovers, ready to make water rescues. An A-6 or A-7 aerial tanker also stays aloft during flight operations so a pilot can refuel in the air. The tanker is always last to land.

For carrier takeoffs, a hissing steam catapult hurls the planes down the deck and into the air at 150 knots (172 mph). A Navy supercarrier like *Carl Vinson* has four catapults. "Cat crews" are able to send up four aircraft in less than a minute.

During flight operations, the carrier deck is very noisy. Jet engines roar and whine. Catapults scream. Crew members, wearing ear protection, communicate with hand and body signals. The best place to observe all this activity is from the superstructure—the "island" rising above the flight deck. From here the air operations officer, known as the air boss, keeps track of what goes on below. Deck crew members wear brightly colored shirts or sweaters to identify their jobs. "Blue shirts," or plane pushers, move aircraft between the flight deck and the hangar deck just below. "Yellow shirts" direct traffic, signalling the pilots where to go after landing. Those who refuel aircraft are "purple shirts," also known as "grapes." "Ordies," in red shirts, load weapons onto planes. Each plane has its own crew of "brown shirts" to check the plane for mechanical problems.

Deck crew members with the most dangerous jobs are the "green shirts"—hookup people and hook runners. Hookup people fasten the tension bar to hold a plane back while the pilot revs the engine to build up power before catapulting

**In an aircraft carrier's Combat Information Center, crew members monitor information being received by various electronic equipment.**

down the deck. Hook runners speed into action when a plane lands. They pull the arresting wire free after the plane has stopped.

The job of a carrier crew is to support aircraft and pilots. About half of the crew are "airdales"—workers connected with aviation. They include deck crew, parachute riggers who inspect and repack the pilots' parachutes, and mechanics and technicians who fix anything that goes wrong with the aircraft.

Elsewhere on a carrier are crew members who oversee the ship's power plant, or who scan radar scopes for thunderstorms or enemy missiles, aircraft, or ships. Technicians in the carrier's Combat Information Center, or CIC, work at computers and operate the electronic equipment

45

WALKERTON ELEMENTARY
SCHOOL LIBRARY

that controls the weapons systems. In the galleys, mess management specialists prepare meals.

For a carrier the size of *Carl Vinson*, that means a lot of cooking. *Carl Vinson*, typical of the Navy's new nuclear-powered carriers, has a crew of nearly 6,000. The ship is 1,092 feet long—almost as long as the Empire State Building is tall! From keel to mast (bottom to the top of the highest pole), the carrier is as high as a 24-story building.

On a ship this large, it is easy to get lost. Miles of passageways crisscross between hundreds of separate, watertight compartments. The carrier is much like a small town—with an airport on the roof! It has storekeepers, doctors, dentists, barbers, a post office, a library, and even a printing plant which puts out a daily newspaper. Sailors can watch closed-circuit television, listen to the ship's radio station, or work

When time allows, crew members can exercise aboard ship— sometimes jogging above deck.

By folding the wings on aircraft, the Navy can store planes close together in a hangar just below the flight deck.

out at a gym. From time to time, when the flight deck is clear, crew members have barbecues on the "steel beach."

Like a city, a carrier has fire hydrants and trained fire fighters. Unlike cities, it also has stations with special foam to put out burning aviation fuel. Almost daily there are fire drills in which everyone takes part.

The larger carriers can store 100 or more planes with their wings folded to make them more compact.

Besides aircraft assigned to carriers, there are Navy planes and helicopters at land bases. They include trainers, cargo transports, aerial tankers, search and rescue craft, and P-3 Orion squadrons that fly on patrol off the Atlantic and Pacific coasts doing weather research and ocean surveillance.

To search for enemy submarines offshore, the 12-person Orion crew drops sonobuoys—three-foot-long devices shaped like coffee cans—that transmit sounds from below the ocean's surface. Often, crews pick up the noises of whales or schools of fish. One of the things they must learn is how not to confuse a whale with a submarine!

A crew member stands in front of a gun aboard the battleship USS *Iowa.* Activated during World War II, the *Iowa* was placed in storage, then reactivated in the mid-1980s.

# 3
# The Surface Navy

There are more than 500,000 men and women in the Navy. At any one time, about half of them are on sea duty while the rest work ashore. Those at sea serve on one of the Navy's 450 ships—either in the "battle force" or its "support force."

Battle force ships are ready to fight in combat if necessary. These are the submarines, large carriers and their escort cruisers, destroyers, and frigates, as well as the smaller helicopter carriers, battleships, minelayers, minesweepers, and amphibious landing craft.

Support force ships are the cargo vessels, troop ships, ammunition ships, and fuel tankers that provide supplies or services. Support force ships also include tenders—the Navy's "floating machine shops" that have metal lathes and other machinery to handle just about any repair job. *Vulcan*, the first Navy vessel on which women served as crew, is a tender. At first, *Vulcan* stayed close to shore while its crew made repairs to other vessels in port. Then in 1979, *Vulcan* was sent to the Mediterranean. There were 66 women among the 730 crew members on that voyage—the first time women sailors went aboard as part of a ship's crew. Women soon began to serve on many surface ships of the fleet. In 1990, one-half of the officers and crew of the Navy tender *Samuel Gompers* were women.

The kind of work a sailor does depends on the vessel to which he or she is assigned. Sailors at the Navy's submarine base in Charleston, South Carolina, work aboard the Navy's mobile floating dry dock, refitting and repairing the submarines that patrol the Atlantic Ocean. Crew members on a missile-armed cruiser may be assigned to the weapons control center, where they punch keys on a computer. The job of a tugboat crew is to help ease huge ships up to piers at stateside naval bases. Storekeepers on supply ships keep track of which supplies go where.

Sometimes deliveries to a ship at sea are not supplies. A delivery might be a sailor reporting for duty or a visitor to the ship. Usually a helicopter brings the person aboard, but a transfer between ships can also be made with a breeches buoy—a metal chair that resembles a ski-lift chair. The breeches buoy glides on a connecting cable stretched from one ship to the other.

Moving people or goods between ships is not easy. The two vessels must travel at exactly the same speed. They must proceed in the same direction, staying a certain number of yards apart so they don't collide. When a ship takes on fuel, its crew shoots a thin cord to a tanker, using a special gun. Once the connection is made, sailors draw the rubber-coated fuel line from the tanker to the ship. Even nuclear-powered carriers depend on tankers to supply fuel for their propeller-driven aircraft, helicopters, and jets.

In earlier times, ships called at a port to stock up on food. Eventually, "replenishment" vessels began to deliver supplies to ships at sea. By getting supplies from replenishment vessels, ships make fewer port calls and can stay at sea longer. Fortunately, sailors are kept so busy that few have the time to be homesick or bored. All crew members have regular duties. The working hours at sea are not always from "eight

**Ships refuel at sea, rather than docking at port for fuel and supplies. The ship on the right is a replenishment oiler refueling the missile cruiser on the left.**

to five." They are "until the job's done"—even if it means working around the clock.

On battle force ships, the gunners, radio operators, and other crew members practice their skills during training exercises, including fleet-wide war games.

Every vessel in the fleet—whether battle or support force—stages regular damage-control drills. Damage control, or DC, is an all-hands responsibility. That means that each sailor must know how to "prevent, minimize, or correct damage from any cause—battle, fire, collision, grounding, explosion...."

Ships schedule regular firefighting drills. Each crew member has a damage-control assignment in addition to his or her regular job. Throughout a ship are lockers with nozzle hoses and protective firefighting gear, including OBA (Oxygen Breathing Apparatus). Close on the heels of the firefighter who goes first into a burning compartment is an "adaptor." This person uses special equipment to keep a wall of water around the firefighter, to protect him or her against intense heat that can reach as high as 1,800 degrees!

In 1988, a fire broke out aboard the carrier *Constellation*. Fed by fuel oil, the fire spread. Suddenly an explosion ripped through the main machinery room. An emergency firefighting squad rushed to fight the blaze.

"There was a fireball...everyone was knocked into the bulkheads [walls]," a squad member said later. "I remember my OBA mask was torn off. The passageway turned orange because of the fire in the air. I smelled hair and flesh burning."

Although the fire took 24 hours to contain, or control, and caused some casualties and much damage, the carrier survived. An emergency squad member gave credit for the squad's quick action to its damage-control training.

"Our training was invaluable to us," he said. "It saved our ship."

Because this kind of training is so important, shipboard firefighting squads—or parties, as they are called—go back to firefighting school often to retrain.

Although sailors aboard ship keep busy, they still have a little free time. Like crew members on aircraft carriers, sailors aboard the Navy's surface ships have access to game rooms, snack counters, libraries, and gyms. They can watch closed-circuit television. When helicopters deliver mail every week or so, they generally bring new movies and television videos. The crew's living quarters—or berthing areas—are

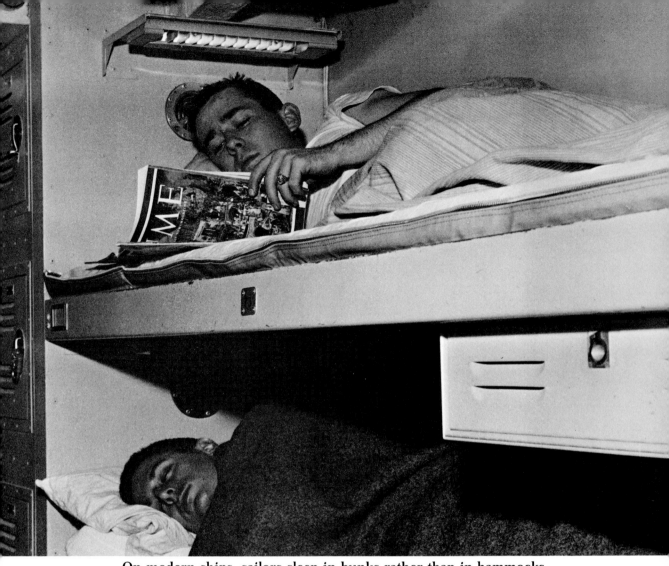

**On modern ships, sailors sleep in bunks rather than in hammocks.**

compact but comfortable. The Navy did away with hammocks almost 50 years ago. Modern-day sailors sleep in bunks. Each bunk has its own reading light, ventilation, built-in locker, and privacy curtain.

Holidays are special times aboard ships. Thanksgiving means traditional roast turkey with all the trimmings and

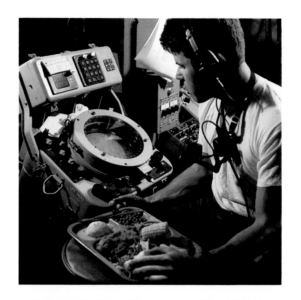

Right: An air controlman eats his Thanksgiving dinner while keeping an eye on the radar in an amphibious assault vessel. Below: Crew members monitor radar screens aboard a battleship. Electronic technology has changed the way the Navy does its work.

pumpkin pie. When the ship crosses the equator—the line on maps and globes that divides the northern and southern hemispheres—sailors celebrate Wog Day, a Navy tradition. Old salts hold court to initiate the "pollywogs"—those who have never crossed the equator before. After a silly ceremony, all in good fun, the pollywog receives a certificate declaring he or she is a "trusty shellback." Even ships' crews zigzagging across the Pacific Ocean in the midst of World War II took time out to celebrate crossing the line.

Modern-day sailors need to know more than how to handle, work, and navigate a ship. They must be sailor-technicians who work with electronics and computers. Modern ships are filled with sophisticated electronic gadgets. The Navy has come a long way from the days of wooden sailing ships, when a powderboy ran from the ship's magazine (ammunition storage area) with bags of gunpowder for sailors firing broadsides from the man-of-war's gundeck. On modern Navy ships, guns are often fully automated. Crews load and fire them by remote control. Missiles have replaced many of the conventional weapons of World War II. A computer operator can strike a key to launch antimissile weapons against enemy missiles or aircraft. These rocket-powered missiles are designed to track and destroy airborne threats, either shooting them down or exploding them before they get to the ship.

Despite new gadgetry, the Navy is strong on old traditions. Uniforms for enlisted men look much like those worn by bluejackets of the 1800s—including the practical bell-bottoms. Every recruit learns at boot camp that those wide trouser legs, when tied at the ends, hold a lot of air. They make a dandy emergency flotation device! Folklore claims the 13

The basic Navy uniform—"Dixie cup" hat and bell-bottom trousers—has remained almost unchanged through the 20th century. This modern-day sailor stands beside the Lone Sailor statue at the U.S. Navy Memorial in Washington, D.C.

buttons on the trouser flap represent the original 13 colonies, although it can't be proved. The sailor's white canvas "Dixie cup" hat dates from 1886. Before then, sailors wore straw hats.

A cherished Navy tradition is the "bo'sun's pipe." The boatswain (bo'sun), with a shrill pipe to relay orders, has always been an important person on a ship. Over the ship's public-address system, the pipe is still used for passing the word. It is used to announce meal time. A sailor who retires from the service is always "piped ashore" with an appropriate ceremony. The boatswain also uses the pipe to announce that a special visitor has come onto the ship.

56

To honor important visitors, the ship's bell may be rung once or twice. Someone really important, such as the president of the United States or the secretary of the Navy, rates a salute of eight bells. Ship's bells also ring every half hour to announce the time. They work up from one bell, at a half hour past midnight, to eight bells at four in the morning. Then the cycle begins again, starting with one bell at half past four, two bells at five in the morning, and so on. (Eight bells are rung at 4:00 A.M., 8:00 A.M., noon, 4:00 P.M., 8:00 P.M., and midnight—or, in Navy time, 0400, 0800, 1200, 1600, 2000, and 2400 hours.) In earlier days, the sailor on watch reported to the captain morning, noon, and night at eight bells to tell him how things were going, such as where the sailing vessel was, which crew members were sick, and how low food supplies were getting. Because tradition is important in the Navy, the quarterdeck watch still seeks out the captain at 2000 hours to give an "eight o'clock report."

Long ago, ships used flags to relay messages to other ships, or to people on shore. At night, they used lights. Although modern ships have wireless radios or radio-telephones, they use flags or lights during a communications "blackout" or when they fear the enemy might intercept a message. For ceremonies, ships hoist international alphabet flags and numeral pennants just as "Old Ironsides" did during its triumphant world cruise many years ago.

# 4
# See the World—
# and Learn A Skill!

Nearly a century ago, the Navy promised adventure to all the people who joined, plus a chance to see the world. If you were to join the modern Navy, you would get that—and a whole lot more. At Navy service schools, you can learn anything from aircraft maintenance and computer programming to cooking and storekeeping. On the job—on a ship or ashore—sailors do the same work civilians do. Sailors repair diesel engines and operate forklifts. They fight fires and take photographs. They are electronic technicians, plumbers, and accountants. They are nuclear power experts, steam fitters, writers, and chefs.

If you want to join the Navy, the first step is to talk with a recruiter. You will learn what it takes to enlist and the kinds of training the Navy offers. Navy recruiters have offices in most cities and they often visit high schools around the country.

The Navy requires that its recruits have a high school diploma and be in good health. You must be at least 58 inches tall (4 feet, 10 inches), but no taller than 78 inches (6 feet, 6 inches). With permission from your parents or guardian, you can join the Navy at 17. Otherwise you must be 18. Recruits can be no older than 34.

When a recruiter talks with you, the first question will probably be about your hobbies, interests, and education.

You will be asked to answer a few sample questions from ASVAB, the Armed Services Vocational Aptitude Battery. This is the standard military test all potential recruits must take. After you answer the sample questions, the recruiter will send you to a testing center to take the complete ASVAB test.

ASVAB questions are multiple-choice and test your mathematical skills, reading comprehension, problem-solving skills, and language abilities. From your scores in each area, the Navy can decide what kind of work you might do well and which training school might be best for you. If you don't pass the ASVAB test the first time, the recruiter may suggest you study some more and retake the test later.

All female recruits, and some male recruits, take basic training in Orlando, Florida. Men planning to go into welding, electronics, or apprenticeship training may go to the Great Lakes Naval Training Center near Chicago, Illinois. Those who will study cooking or communications after boot camp usually take basic training at the Navy base in San Diego, California.

Basic training begins with a physical exam, shots, and a haircut. A woman recruit may have an individual hairstyle, as long as her hair does not overlap her collar. Male recruits receive a standard Navy cut: barbers work fast, and they don't leave much hair above the skin covering the skull.

At boot camp, recruits begin a whole new way of life. As soon as they stand at attention in that first formation, they know that they are in the Navy, now! Recruits quickly learn what discipline is all about. From the day they enter boot camp, they must be up at 4:30 A.M. By 9:30 or 10:00 P.M., it's "lights out."

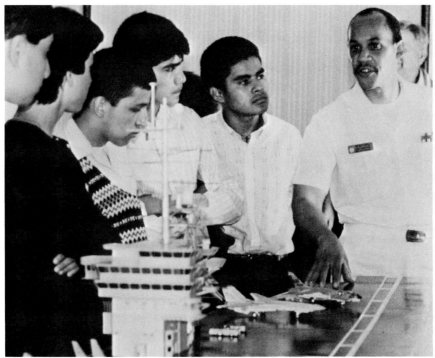

Navy recruiters use a table-top model of an aircraft carrier to explain flight deck operations to high school students. Recruiters are knowledgeable about most aspects of Navy life and can help potential recruits decide if they want to join the Navy.

Navy standards are high. From the start, recruits learn to obey orders, to be on time for formations, to wear the proper uniform, and to be prepared for any task they are assigned.

At boot camp, recruits learn techniques for survival at sea. Navy recruits must know how to swim. For the basic test you won't have to paddle fast or far, but you must demonstrate to the Navy that you can stay afloat.

As has been the rule for decades, men and women at boot camp must wear leggings, called boots, until the last week of basic training. They wear the boots when doing work in dungaree jeans and also when wearing dress uniforms — either in white pants and shirts for summer or in their winter "blues."

Basic training lasts eight to nine weeks. During that time, each recruit learns the things every bluejacket has to know about seamanship, ship structures, naval customs, and naval traditions. On a Navy ship, the entire crew has to learn to work together. Therefore, an important part of boot camp is doing things as a team. Another vital part of training is learning to cope with emergencies, such as fires and poison gas leaks.

Navy personnel must become good at dealing with emergency situations. A small group tries to contain the damage caused by a broken water pipe in a training exercise.

Graduation day is exciting for everyone. Recruits' families are invited to watch the ceremony as the recruits take part in a full parade. Boot camp graduates have gained a higher status. No longer are they raw recruits, scared and unsure of themselves like the lowly "booties" just entering boot camp.

Once out of boot camp, recruits can either take more training at a service—or technical—school, or they can opt for on-the-job training. Recruits who choose apprentice-type jobs will take a few more weeks of basic training after boot camp. Then they report to a ship for sea duty and a job such as working in food service, ladling out food in the mess hall. If the sailor does not like the work, he or she can apply for a transfer later.

Graduates of boot camp who go on to Class A service schools will learn the basic skills in their areas of specialty. For more serious study in a chosen area, the sailor then goes on to a Class C school, perhaps to learn advanced electronics.

During training at damage control school, sailors experience an emergency—without the danger. In a trainer unit, like the compartment of a ship, students slosh in water up to their shoulders while more water pours in through a leak in a pipe. Instructors stand by to guide trainees as they struggle to patch the broken pipe. This kind of hands-on class work prepares Navy men and women to face real trouble if it occurs on a ship. At firefighting sessions, students learn how to control shipboard fires that start from sources such as electric wires, weapons, or jet fuel. During training, the environment is controlled, but the fires to be put out are very real.

The Navy's cooking school in San Diego provides sailors

**Musically inclined recruits may join a Navy band.**

with hands-on training of a different sort. In well-equipped kitchens, future cooks and chefs learn all about making pies, cakes, and other tasty and nourishing things to eat.

The Navy has more than 100 basic or advanced technical schools. The training those schools offer leads to jobs in some 60 different career fields. You could study to be a corpsman (an enlisted person who gives first aid and limited medical treatment) at a stateside hospital, an air traffic controller in an aircraft squadron, or an electronics technician on a surface ship. You could even be a bandsman and play in one of the Navy's bands.

Many Navy jobs are like jobs in the civilian world. If you were to leave the Navy after one or two hitches, you could apply your training and skills to a similar civilian job. A damage controller could work as a firefighter, plumber, or welder. A data processing technician, who keeps records

64

up-to-date for the Navy, could become a computer programmer. An aerographer's mate, who observes and forecasts weather information, might do the same thing in civilian life. A hull technician, who repairs ships, could be a welder, steamfitter, plumber, or carpenter.

Besides good starting pay, with raises as recruits move up to supervisor-level positions, the Navy offers these benefits:
- housing and meals
- medical and dental care
- extra pay for certain types of duty
- 30 days of paid vacation every year, regardless of rank or length of service
- full pay and allowances during training and while attending Navy schools
- free travel on military flights to military bases
- retirement pay after 20 years of service

You can enlist in the Navy for three, four, five, or six years of active duty, depending on the program you select. Sailors who are not assigned permanently to shore duty will alternate between three years of sea duty and three years ashore.

Submarine duty is open to male volunteers only. Each recruit goes through a series of tests and interviews to make sure he is qualified. A submariner must be quick and active, both mentally and physically. Not everyone can take the stress of living with others in such close quarters, and of staying submerged for a week or more with no chance to come to the surface and see the sun or stars.

Since most of the Navy's submarines are nuclear-powered, crews learn about nuclear energy and operation of nuclear power plants. During training, students practice in submarine simulators that have dials and controls like those on an actual sub. The compartment can be tilted up, down, or sideways. After the vessel "submerges" to a certain depth, a fixture bursts in a controlled emergency situation, and students must locate and seal the breaks with clamps. In an escape-training tank, submariners learn how to escape from a submerged sub.

With all the studying required, a submarine crewman may not see his first sea duty for two years. An officer may spend up to three years getting ready for the job.

Male and female candidates for Navy diving school are also volunteers. They, too, need special skills and must be in excellent physical condition. They can expect tough physical training—running, swimming, and climbing obstacle courses—every day. After training, divers may be assigned to take underwater photographs or work on underwater wrecks. They may have to retrieve equipment dropped over the side of a vessel or be part of a construction team.

The diver program called BUD/SEAL (*B*asic *U*nderwater *D*emolition/*Sea*, *A*ir, and *L*and, is open to men only, since some of its activities are related to combat. "SEALS" are the most highly trained and most disciplined of the Navy divers. Like those of the frogmen and underwater commandos in World War II, BUD/SEAL missions are secret.

Both men and women may become pilots. A pilot candidate must be no older than 24, in excellent health with good eyesight. A pilot must have a four-year college degree and must be a commissioned officer. (A Navy commission may be earned at Naval Academy, Annapolis; through Naval Reserve Officers Training Corps [NROTC] at college; or at Aviation Officer Candidate School [AOCS] in Pensacola, Florida.)

The pilot program begins with classroom work and tough

Left: Sea-Air-Land (SEAL) team members in a life raft follow an amphibious assault vehicle after completing a training exercise. Right: A diver prepares to enter the water for a training exercise in finding and detonating explosives. BUD/SEAL divers have been responsible in wartime for disabling mines set out by enemy forces.

physical training. Then students spend between 1 and 1½ years at flight school in Pensacola, learning to fly jet and propeller aircraft or helicopters.

After graduation from flight school, some Navy pilots may serve with land bases to ferry aircraft, instruct pilot candidates, fly search and rescue missions, or serve with P-3 Orion surveillance squadrons. But most pilots join carrier

A P-3 Orion aircraft makes a sharp turn during a flight. The plane is one of many the Navy trains its pilots to fly.

squadrons for six months of duty. Then they return to shore for a year or more of training. During that year, a few lucky pilots may attend Top Gun, the Navy Fighter Weapons School at Miramar, California. Here they learn tactics to teach fellow pilots when they return to their fleet squadrons on carriers.

Navy regulations require that sailors stay in good physical condition. All sailors—including officers—must take a physical readiness test twice a year. They have to do sit-ups, push-ups, take a stretching test, and do a timed run or swim.

Throughout a sailor's career, schooling can continue. Navy men and women are encouraged to "Move UP, Not Out. Stay

Navy!" Aboard ship, sailors can study correspondence courses on their own to increase their knowledge, or to gain a higher rating. Crew members of many ships can take university-level courses under programs like PACE (Program for Afloat College Education). Most PACE courses are college freshman and sophomore level and are taught by qualified professors traveling with the Navy.

Active duty sailors in the "Navy Campus" program may attend college full-time. Once they get their degrees, they must promise to stay in the Navy for a certain length of time afterward. One program offers an associate of arts or science degree. Another gives enlisted men and women a chance to finish college and then earn a Navy commission through Officer Candidate School.

Midshipmen walk to class at the U.S. Naval Academy near
Annapolis, Maryland.

70

# 5
# The U.S. Naval Academy

When it was suggested in the early 1800s that young Navy officers should study at a school, the old-timers scoffed. "Let them learn by doing," they said. If a midshipman kept his eyes open, he'd learn what he needed to know! Sending him to school ashore, claimed one critic, was like "trying to teach ducks to swim in a garret [attic]."

Congress agreed. So until 1845, the Navy had no academy to train its officers. Then Secretary of the Navy George Bancroft acted on his own, choosing a site near the city of Annapolis, Maryland, 33 miles from Baltimore and 33 miles from Washington. It was a fort where the Severn River flows into Chesapeake Bay, so students would have plenty of water for learning seamanship.

The U.S. Naval Academy at Annapolis eventually grew to offer four years of basic education and practical study. Graduates earn a bachelor of science degree and a commission as a Navy ensign or as a second lieutenant in the Marines. The academy provides money for uniforms and books. It also pays for the midshipman's tuition, medical and dental care, and room and board. In return, a midshipman agrees to serve at least five years on active military duty after graduation. Most choose to serve well beyond five years. Since 1976, women have attended the academy. They make up over 10 percent of the total brigade, or student body, of almost 4,300. Regardless of gender, all students attending the Naval Academy are called midshipmen.

To enter the academy, you must be between 17 and 22 years old and have no dependents. You must be healthy with normal vision, and a U.S. citizen of good moral character. The Naval Academy wants young people who will make good leaders. A high grade point average during high school is important, but good grades alone are not enough. Students should also excel in athletics and be active in school clubs, student government, community service, or scouting. They need to be able to communicate well with others. Besides the other requirements, applicants must pass a rigorous physical fitness test. It includes pull-ups for men or fixed arm hang for women, a 300-yard shuttle run, a kneeling basketball throw, and a standing long jump.

Competition to enter the academy is fierce. Applicants must be nominated—usually by members of Congress—and approved by the academy. Each year the academy admits a few enlisted men and women from the regular Navy or Marines or the naval reserves who have completed a year of study at NAPS (the U.S. Naval Academy Preparatory School) in Newport, Rhode Island.

Freshmen, called plebes, begin their four-year program at the academy with Plebe Summer. Most midshipmen agree that the hardest time of all is Plebe Summer. It begins with Induction Day in early July, when, as one midshipman explains, "they cut your hair and send your clothes home in a box." From then on, plebes learn to speak in nautical and academy terms. The floor is a deck, walls are bulkheads, the rest room is the head. For the next seven weeks, plebes start their days at dawn with an hour of running, sit-ups, and push-ups. They rush from swimming to sailing, to a lecture, then to lunch. There are classes in first aid. At the weapons

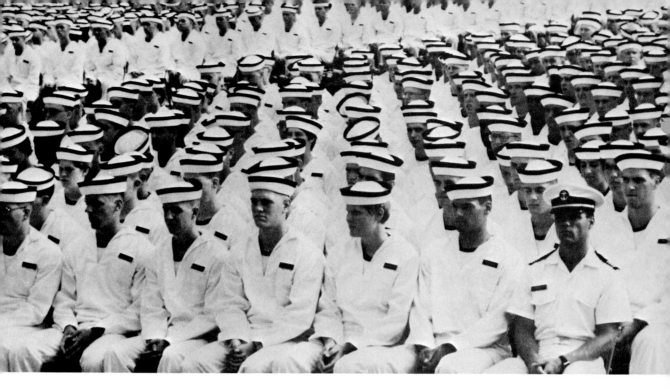

Above: Plebes await the swearing-in ceremony shortly after arriving at the Naval Academy. Plebes can be easily identified by the dark blue band that circles the top of their "Dixie cup" hats. Right: George Bancroft, secretary of the Navy when the Naval Academy was founded, was responsible for starting a school to train sailors. When Bancroft was unable to secure support for an academy, he added programs slowly and on his own. Years later, he had added so many programs that government officials were forced to recognize that he had started a school, which was to become the U.S. Naval Academy.

73

**A plebe receives instructions on the weapons range.**

range, they learn to fire small arms safely and accurately. During that first summer, each plebe must buy and master his or her own personal computer. The frantic pace continues each day until long after sunset. All the while, plebes have to take orders from practically everyone.

This exhausting schedule has a purpose. It helps plebes to reach top physical condition. It teaches them to manage their time, to decide which things are most important. One midshipman says the best feature about Plebe Summer for her was "how we all pulled together... women were expected to do just what the men did. It was hard, but everyone cheered me on if I fell behind, and there was always a helping hand."

Plebes have to remind themselves of a saying that reflects the value of working hard: "If you don't try, you don't make it.

If you do try, you will make it." About 75 percent of them do.

Regular class work begins in the fall. Besides studies in their major field—engineering, science, mathematics, social sciences, or the humanities—students learn about navigation, naval engineering, weapons, leadership, and naval history. Classes are small, with between 10 and 27 students. The work is hard. Although most students were among the best in their own high schools, so were those with whom they compete for grades at the Naval Academy. All midshipmen have to push themselves beyond their old limits. This is part of what it will take to meet the challenge of being a naval officer later on.

Besides academic classes, every midshipman must take four years of physical education and also take part in a competitive varsity or intramural sport each season. The reason? To learn teamwork, leadership, and how to cope

**Midshipmen attend classes in a variety of subjects.**

**Participation in competitive sports, like the rowing team, is mandatory for midshipmen.**

under stress. There are 33 varsity and 23 intramural sports offered—from basketball, crew (rowing), fencing, and gymnastics to volleyball, water polo, and wrestling.

Extracurricular activities (ECAs) are encouraged. Midshipmen can box or join the drum and bugle corps. They can sing in a choir, staff a radio station, or help put out the yearbook or the humor magazine. There are clubs for those interested in art, drama, photography, parachute jumping, scuba diving, and more.

With all the study and physical activity, it is no wonder a typical day's diet adds up to some 4,500 calories. Meals are served family style in a large dining room in Bancroft Hall. The entire brigade eats at the same time, sitting at long tables heaped with such foods as home-baked breads, rolls, pastries, steak, spiced shrimp, steamed Chesapeake crabs, and homemade ice cream!

The brigade is divided into 36 companies. Each company has its own living area at Bancroft Hall. Usually two or three

76

women, or two or three men share a dormitory room. Company mates live, eat, study, drill, play, and compete together as teams, so they get a first-hand lesson in teamwork.

Like the rest of the Navy, the academy is strong on tradition. In front of Bancroft Hall stands a statue of a Native American whom midshipmen have come to call "Tecumseh." His other nickname is "God of the 2.5." Those about to take exams toss pennies in the quiver holding his arrows to make sure they get at least a passing, or 2.5, grade! To ensure

A midshipman passes Tecumseh. The statue was originally a wooden figurehead attached to the front of the USS *Delaware*. Then it was removed from the ship and placed in a courtyard at the academy. Eventually, when it began to rot, the wooden figurehead was replaced by a bronze replica, or copy.

a victory when the Navy team meets its arch foe, Army, midshipmen splash red, yellow, and white war paint on Tecumseh's war bonnet and tomahawk. On their way to the game, they give the old statue a left-hand salute and toss coins in the quiver for good luck.

Sure to be at the game is Bill the Goat, the academy mascot. He is led by first-classmen (seniors) who earned the honor by getting good grades and top marks in military drill and athletics. (Besides the special privilege of leading the mascot, these first-classmen carry flags in parades and special events.)

If Navy does beat Army in the football game, midshipmen ring the Japanese Bell in the entrance to Bancroft Hall—one stroke for each point scored! The very old bell was a gift from Commodore Matthew Perry, who received it from the Japanese in 1854.

Around the academy, midshipmen see many reminders of the Navy's history. Monuments honor brave deeds of Navy heroes, like Captain William Herndon, who went down with his ship in a hurricane off Cape Hatteras in 1857. Murals in Bancroft Hall depict famous naval battles. Walkways and buildings such as Rickover Hall and Nimitz Library are named for graduates who contributed to U. S. naval history. Memorial Hall contains hundreds of mementos, including Commodore Oliver Perry's battle flag with the words "Don't Give Up the Ship" sewn onto the fabric, the flag flown by the ironclad *Monitor*, the kedge anchor *Constitution*'s Captain Hull used to escape from the British in 1812, and the coat John Paul Jones wore when *Bonhomme Richard* fought the British frigate *Serapis*. The academy is also the burial place of John Paul Jones, whose crypt is located beneath the chapel.

Every year, plebes of the Naval Academy pool their efforts to retrieve a plebe hat from atop the Herndon Monument. Older midshipmen smear the monument with lard to make the task more difficult.

The school year ends with Commission Week in May. Graduates receive their commissions as naval officers—and plebes have their last chance to work as a team. As one plebe observed, "There are two main points in a midshipman's career—Herndon and graduation!"

"Herndon" is a 21-foot-high monument. Upper classmen set a plebe's white "Dixie cup" hat atop it, and then grease the tall marble shaft with 200 pounds of lard. After that, plebes must scale the monument and rescue the hat. If they don't succeed, academy legend says they will remain plebes forever. The team begins by scraping away the slippery, slimy lard. A few plebes circle the monument, arms linked. A few more scramble to stand on the shoulders of those in the first layer. Onlookers shout. Arms wave. The human pyramid

Graduation ceremonies at the Naval Academy always end with the graduates tossing their hats into the air.

grows higher until one plebe pushes high enough to reach the top, grab the hat, and replace it with the hat of an upperclassman. More cheers! Legend also has it that the one who rescues the hat will be the first admiral of the class.

Other activities of Commission Week include dances, parties, parades, and concerts. The academy sailing squadron stages a regatta. On graduation day, the Blue Angels—the Navy's precision flying team—mark the special time with a stunning flight demonstration. After the diplomas are awarded, the graduates give "three cheers for those we leave behind!" A thousand caps fly into the air—to land who knows where? But that's all right. These new officers will need their midshipmen's caps no longer.

Some of them will enter the Marines. Others will head for Pensacola to become naval aviators, or they will be assigned to a ship of the surface Navy. A few may study engineering at the Navy's graduate school in Monterey, California, or at another university. Some will go on to submarine school or to take nuclear-power training.

For the undergraduates at the academy, summer is cruise time. Next year's seniors will work as junior officers on a surface warship, submarine, aircraft carrier, or with a land-based aviation patrol squadron. For those who will be second-classmen (juniors) in the fall, the cruise will introduce them to every major branch of the Navy and Marines. They will fly in Navy aircraft, go on patrol with the Marines, and dive in a nuclear-powered submarine. Ex-plebes, next year's third-classmen, will take the "youngster" cruise. As part of the crew of a Navy ship or submarine, they will work at gunnery exercises and stand watches. This will give them a feel for how things seem from the viewpoint of enlisted men and women.

Among the academy's graduates are Albert A. Michelson, class of 1873, first American scientist to win the Nobel prize; former President Jimmy Carter, class of 1946; and more than 25 Rhodes scholars. Thirty NASA mission specialists and astronauts were Annapolis graduates, as were five members of the United States team at the 1988 Olympics in South Korea. At the time of World War II, nearly all regular Navy officers, including Admirals William Leahy, Ernest King, Chester Nimitz, William Halsey, Raymond Spruance, and Arleigh Burke, had attended the academy.

Many graduates find it hard to put in words the tangibles and intangibles the academy gave them. Their time there was more than just an education. Deeds of past naval heroes inspired the officers and made them proud. The physical training built strength, agility, and endurance. The military environment encouraged self-discipline.

Vice Admiral James B. Stockdale, who graduated from the academy in 1946, was a naval aviator in the Vietnam War. After his plane was shot down, he was one of the first Americans to be taken prisoner. His personal conduct as senior prisoner of war for seven years, and the way he resisted torture, isolation, and brutal treatment, set an example for his fellow prisoners. Stockdale has said his ability to resist torture and to perform far beyond the call of duty came from his Naval Academy training.

# 6
# Looking Ahead

In 200 years, the United States Navy grew from a cluster of wooden ships and a few sailors seeking adventure on the high seas, to a powerful fighting force. Its nuclear-powered ships and submarines can travel for years without refueling. Supersonic Navy aircraft can find and track targets without ever seeing them. In the years ahead, Navy researchers will develop equipment and techniques that are even more complex.

**By keeping ships offshore and prepared for battle, the Navy hopes to keep governments and other military groups from threatening the United States or its allies with physical harm.**

The salute: an important
military tradition

But even as the Navy advances and makes changes, it will keep its old traditions. Customs and courtesies around which it developed are very much a part of Navy life.

The naval custom observed most often is the salute. Saluting is a courtesy that military forces have practiced for centuries. In the Navy, enlisted personnel salute officers. All Navy men and women salute the ship's flag, called the ensign, when they board or leave a ship. Each sailor also salutes the officer of the deck when requesting permission to come aboard or to leave the ship. When granting that permission, the officer of the deck returns the salute.

Something else that will remain the same in the years ahead is the Navy's mission. Like the other branches of the armed forces, the Navy is committed to defending the nation in time of war.

The Navy has a second mission—one that is just as important. And that is to help keep the peace. It is one reason Navy ships and aircraft deploy to other parts of the world. The Navy shows a United States presence. The hope is that nations or groups threatening to make trouble will be less likely to disturb the peace if they see the power of the United States fleet offshore and ready.

# Appendix

In the United States Navy, personnel hold different ranks or grades. *Commissioned officers* have earned their positions by completing course work at the Naval Academy, through the Naval Reserve Officers Training Corps, or at the Aviation Officer Candidate School. After completing one of these programs, a person receives a commission. *Noncommissioned officers* are enlisted personnel (those who sign up with a recruiter) who have obtained their positions by earning promotions throughout their careers in the Navy, starting as seamen recruits.

*Commissioned Officers*
Admiral
Vice Admiral
Rear Admiral
Rear Admiral (Lower Half)
Captain
Commander
Lieutenant Commander
Lieutenant
Lieutenant Junior Grade
Ensign
Chief Warrant Officer

*Enlisted Personnel*
Warrant Officer
Master Chief Petty Officer
Senior Chief Petty Officer
Chief Petty Officer
Petty Officer First Class
Petty Officer Second Class
Petty Officer Third Class
Seaman
Seaman Apprentice
Seaman Recruit

# Index

*Photo Credits*

Most of the photographs that appear in this book are courtesy of the United
States Navy. Navy photographs by unknown photographers: pp. 6, 13 (from oil
painting by Birch), 18, 35, 36, 37, 47, 53, and 73 (bottom). Photographs provided
by the United States Navy and taken by named photographers or originating
from known sources: pp. 1, 48, 83, PH1 Jeff Hilton; 8, Sikorsky Aircraft; 10, U.S.
Naval Academy Museum (from painting by Cecelia Beaux); 12, PH3 N.C. Barrett
(from oil painting by William Elliott); 16, PH2 (AC) Scott M. Allen; 17, PH2 Karl
G. Zettel; 22, JOC Fred J. Klinkenberger; 25, 28, U.S. Army; 26, 41, U.S. Naval
Historical Center; 29, PHAN John G. Jacob; 30, Gerald Lepone; 32, Lt. Cmdr.
John Leenhouts; 38, PH1 Harold J. Gerwien; 39, 51, 58, PH1 Chuck Mussi; 42,
PH3 Douglas E. Houser; 43, PH2 Carl Duvall; 45, PH2 Gary P. Bonaccorso; 46, 54
(top), PH2 (SW) Jeffrey A. Elliott; 54 (bottom), International Defense Images;
56, JOCS Adams; 61, JO1 Jim Bryant; 62, Tom Milne; 64, PH2 Don Koralewski;
67 (left), Master Sgt. Stephen B. Jones; 67 (right), PH1 Larry Franklin, USNR
(Ret.); 68, Mark Meyer; 70, 73 (top), W.R. McCrea; 76, PH1 E.G. Norris; 77,
PHAN M.D. Porter; 80, T. Darden; and 84, PH3 E.G. Nicciolo, Jr.

Other photographs are courtesy of: pp. 2, 19, Library of Congress; 15, Architect
of the Capitol (from painting by William H. Powell); 20, Independent Picture
Service; 74, U.S. Naval Academy; 75, U.S. Naval Academy/D.B. Eckard; and 79,
U.S. Naval Academy/K.J. Mierzejewski.

*Cover photographs are courtesy of the United States Navy. Front cover photograph
by PH3 Douglas E. Houser; back cover photograph by PH1 Michael D.P. Flynn.*